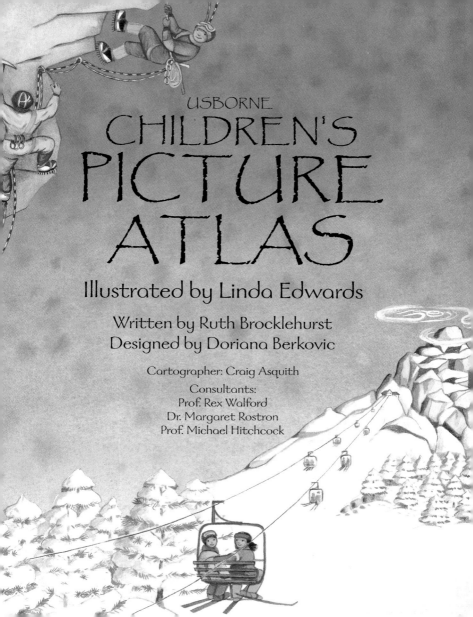

USBORNE

CHILDREN'S PICTURE ATLAS

Illustrated by Linda Edwards

Written by Ruth Brocklehurst
Designed by Doriana Berkovic

Cartographer: Craig Asquith

Consultants:
Prof. Rex Walford
Dr. Margaret Rostron
Prof. Michael Hitchcock

Contents

The Universe

We live in a Universe that's so enormous it's almost impossible to imagine. To picture it, you need to start small, then think big.

Towns and cities

People live in all kinds of places around the world. Most people live in houses or apartments in towns. Really big towns are called cities.

A town has streets with houses, shops, schools and other buildings.

Countries

The land around the world is divided into different countries. Countries usually have towns, cities, farmland and wild countryside.

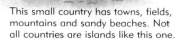

This small country has towns, fields, mountains and sandy beaches. Not all countries are islands like this one.

Planet Earth

A country is just a small part of the land on the planet Earth. The Earth is a huge ball of rock floating in space. Land covers part of it and the rest is sea.

The Sun is a star. It gives out light and heat.

 Mercury

Earth

Venus

Jupiter

Mars

Uranus

 Neptune

Pluto

Saturn

This picture shows all the planets in the Solar System.

The Solar System

The Earth is one of nine planets that go around the Sun. Together, the Sun and these planets are called the Solar System. The Earth is the only planet where people, plants and animals live.

The Universe

There are trillions of stars shining in space and the Sun is one of them. A large group of stars is called a galaxy. The Sun belongs to a galaxy called the Milky Way. All the galaxies in space make up the Universe.

On a clear night, you can see thousands of stars.

5

What are maps?

Maps are pictures that show places as they look from above. They usually make places look much smaller than they really are. A book, like this one, full of maps is called an atlas.

Spacecraft called satellites are used to take photographs of the Earth from space.

This is a satellite photograph. It shows part of London.

Making maps

Mapmakers often use photographs of places taken from above to help them draw maps. They also measure the ground to find out the sizes of places and how far they are from each other.

What maps show

When mapmakers draw maps, they just include the important details. Maps often have shading, labels and little pictures to tell you more about a place.

This is a picture map of the same place as the photograph above.

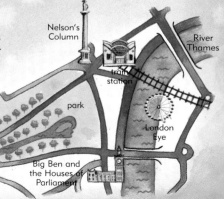

Nelson's Column

River Thames

train station

park

London Eye

Buckingham Palace

Big Ben and the Houses of Parliament

The round Earth

Because the Earth is a ball shape, a photograph can only show one side of it. Mapmakers can show the whole Earth, as it actually looks, by making a model of it. A model Earth is called a globe.

This satellite photograph shows one side of the Earth from space.

If the surface of a globe could be peeled off, this is how it would look.

Peeled Earth

To make a flat map of the round Earth, mapmakers draw the Earth as though its curved surface has been peeled off and opened out flat.

Filling the gaps

The peeled map isn't much use because it has lots of gaps. Some parts have to be squashed or stretched to make a map without gaps.

This is a peeled map. You can see a world map without gaps on pages 28–29.

Countries and cities

There are more than 190 countries in the world. The place where one country meets another is called a border. On the maps in this book, the borders are shown as red dotted lines.

Borders

Many country borders are along rivers or mountains. Sometimes, borders are marked by fences or walls.

Some borders have gates where guards check who goes in and out.

Papua New Guinea has more than 700 islands like this.

Island groups

Some countries, such as Papua New Guinea, are made up of lots of islands. The maps in this book show their borders in the sea around the islands.

Can you find these things on the maps?

Big Ben

Parthenon

St. Basil's Cathedral

Forbidden City

Eiffel Tower

Big cities

Big cities can be very crowded. Many people work or live in tall buildings called skyscrapers. The black circles ● on the maps show where the biggest cities are.

Skyscrapers can fit many hundreds of people into a small space.

This is the White House, in Washington DC, USA. The President of the USA lives and works here.

Country capitals

The people in charge of a country work in a city called the capital. Lots of capitals have big, grand buildings. Capital cities are shown as black squares ■.

Street parties

In some cities, there are street parties called carnivals. People dress up and dance in the streets.

At carnivals, people wear bright, fancy costumes.

Blue Mosque

Winter Palace in St. Petersburg

Leaning Tower of Pisa

Sydney Opera House

Statue of Liberty

9

People

Millions and millions of people live around the world. In different parts of the world, people may look, talk and behave differently.

Japanese children wear kimonos for festivals and special occasions.

Dressing up

In some places, people dress up for special occasions in a style of clothes that people wore long ago. The clothes they wear are called traditional costumes.

Religions

A religion is a way of thinking about the world. Some people believe in one God and others believe in many gods. Most religions have holy places or buildings where people go to pray or think.

In Jerusalem, in Israel, there are many places where Christians, Muslims and Jewish people go to pray.

Can you find these people on the maps?

Guarani people

Zulu dancer

sitar player

rugby player

highland piper

Music and dancing

Many countries have their own styles of music and dancing. Some places have their own traditional musical instruments too.

Flamenco is a Spanish style of dancing to guitar music.

Eating

People around the world eat all kinds of foods. They also have many ways of cooking and eating. Food is transported long distances, so people can taste dishes from all around the world.

Chinese people often eat using chopsticks.

Sharing interests

Although people can be very different, they also have lots in common. With travel, television, telephones and the Internet, it's easy for people to share ideas.

People from all around the world get together to play soccer.

conga drummer

Tibetan monks

Hopi dancer

girl in a poncho

American football player

Getting around

There are many ways to get from one place to another. Journeys can be made by air, land or water. Some are quicker than others.

Jumbo jet planes can carry more than 600 people.

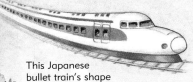

This Japanese bullet train's shape helps it go faster.

Long distances

Planes and trains can carry lots of people at a time. They make long journeys, at great speeds, all around the world.

River rides

It is difficult to build roads in thick forests. The easiest way to travel there is along a river.

Many people canoe along the Amazon River.

Can you find these things on the maps?

basket boat

desert truck

traditional junk (boat)

Trans-Siberian Express

helicopter

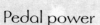

Pedal power

In the busy city streets of India and China, many people use bicycles and rickshaws, instead of cars.

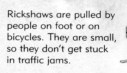

Rickshaws are pulled by people on foot or on bicycles. They are small, so they don't get stuck in traffic jams.

Children can ride on the back of a snowmobile.

Icy journeys

In snowy places, people use snowmobiles and sleds to get around. Snowmobiles have skis, instead of wheels, so they glide easily over the snow.

Watery city

A canal is a man-made river. In Venice, in Italy, there are canals instead of roads. People there use boats to get around the city.

Many people in Venice ride in boats called gondolas. They use poles to push the gondolas along.

Ice and snow

The white parts of the maps show places that are covered with ice and snow. The coldest places in the world are the Arctic in the north and Antarctica in the south.

Arctic terns spend half the year in the Arctic and the other half in Antarctica.

The poles

The most northern place on Earth is called the North Pole. Whichever way you go from there is south. The South Pole is on the other side of the world.

Poles apart

Penguins and polar bears never meet in the wild. This is because penguins live in Antarctica and polar bears only live in the Arctic.

Penguins huddle together to keep out the cold.

Polar bears have thick fur to keep them warm.

Can you find these things on the maps?

ice fish

humpback whale

American science station

Arctic fox

Saami people

These Inuit children are dressed in traditional parkas.

Keeping warm

People in frozen lands need to wrap up warm outside. Inuit people, who live in the Arctic, wear thick coats called parkas to keep out the cold.

Science in the snow

Antarctica is a large, cold island. There, scientists from all over the world work in science stations. They go there to study the weather and to find out about the animals that live there.

Scientists can measure how cold it is in the sky by fixing a thermometer to a weather balloon.

Icebreaker ships are strong and heavy. They break up the frozen ocean, clearing a way for other ships.

Frozen sea

There isn't any land at the North Pole, but much of the sea is frozen solid all year. In the summer, some of the ice melts and breaks up into huge chunks called icebergs.

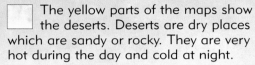

Deserts

The yellow parts of the maps show the deserts. Deserts are dry places which are sandy or rocky. They are very hot during the day and cold at night.

Flamingos flying over the Atacama Desert.

In sandy deserts, wind blows the sand into hills called dunes.

Desert records

The Sahara, in Africa, is the biggest, hottest desert in the world. The driest desert is the Atacama, in Chile. In parts, it hasn't rained for 400 years.

Oasis

An oasis is a place in the desert where there is water. Plants grow there and animals and people go there to drink.

These people are collecting water from an oasis.

Can you find these animals on the maps?

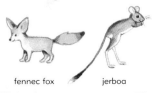

fennec fox

jerboa

blue-tongued skink

scorpion

rattlesnake

Thirsty animals

Camels can drink lots of water at once, then go for a week without any. They are suited to life in the desert in other ways too.

Camels can close their nostrils to stop sand from blowing in.

They have wide feet so they don't sink into the sand.

Plant survival

Desert plants have different ways of surviving in such dry places.

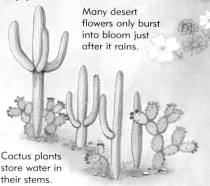

Many desert flowers only burst into bloom just after it rains.

Cactus plants store water in their stems.

Desert people

Many desert people don't live in one place. They move around with their animals, to find water and food.

Bedouins are desert people. Some of them live in camps like this.

Grasslands

Grasslands are flat, open spaces where lots of grasses grow. They are shaded in pale green on the maps. Different types of grasses grow in different places around the world.

Safaris

The grassland in Africa is called the savanna. In the hot, dry season, the grass is dry and golden. People go on tours called safaris to see the wild animals that live there.

Lions spend most of their time resting.

Eating grass

Many savanna animals, such as zebras and antelopes, are grass-eaters. They live in large groups so they are safer from hunters, such as lions.

A group of zebras is called a herd.

Can you find these animals on the maps?

kangaroos

guanaco

buffalo

giraffe

meerkats

Green, green grass

In Northern Europe and New Zealand, the weather is often cool and rainy. The grass there is lush and green and good for cows and sheep to eat.

Farmers get wool and meat from sheep.

Cowboys called gauchos round up cows on horseback.

The pampas

The grassland in South America is called the pampas. Farmers there keep thousands of cows on farms called ranches. Cows are kept for meat and milk.

Grassland farming

Most of the world's wheat and corn grows on the grasslands in Russia and North America. Farmers there use big machines to collect the grain.

Combine harvesters are huge machines that cut wheat and other crops.

lion

giant anteater

African elephant

oryx

rhea

Forests

The dark green parts of the maps show where forests are. Different types of forests grow in different parts of the world.

Conifer trees grow seed cones that squirrels eat.

Conifer trees

Coniferous forests grow in cold places, with snowy winters. Conifer trees have long, thin leaves, called needles. They stay green all year round.

Tropical rainforests

More kinds of plants live in rainforests than anywhere else.

Rainforests grow in parts of the world where it is hot and rainy all the time. They are steamy places with towering trees, thick bushes and millions of animals.

Can you find these things on the maps?

blue morpho butterfly

armadillo

red fox

raccoon

anaconda

Trees in winter

In places with mild weather, many trees lose their leaves in the winter. The leaves turn red and golden before they fall.

The winter wind blows dead leaves from the trees.

In the spring, fresh green leaves grow.

How old is a tree?

You can find out the age of a tree by counting the number of rings in its trunk. A tree has a ring for each year of its life.

When a tree is cut down, you can see the rings in its trunk.

Giant pandas only eat bamboo.

Forests of bamboo

Giant pandas live in bamboo forests, in the mountains of China. There, the bamboo grows tall and thick. Only around 600 giant pandas live in the wild.

grizzly bear

wild mushrooms

lumberjack (forester)

chimpanzee

toucan

Mountains

Mountains are high, rocky places. Their highest points are called peaks. Tiny mountain shapes on the maps show where the biggest mountains are.

Ski lifts take skiers up and down mountains.

Snowy peaks

The higher up a mountain you go, the colder and windier it gets. On the high slopes, it is too cold for trees to grow. The highest peaks are so cold that they are covered with snow, even in the summer.

Snow leopards have pale fur, to blend in with their snowy surroundings.

Climbing creatures

Many mountain animals, such as goats and snow leopards, are excellent climbers. They also have extra-thick fur to keep out the chilly winds.

Mighty mountains

A line of mountains is called a range. The Andes, in South America, is the longest mountain range in the world.

Some farmers in the Andes keep llamas for their wool.

Climbers use ropes and hooks to help them cling onto rocky ledges upside down.

Climbing

Mount Everest is the highest mountain in the world. Many adventurers travel to Asia to make the difficult climb to its highest peak.

Mountain birds

Some birds, such as eagles and condors, live high up in mountains. They build their nests on rocky cliffs and narrow ledges.

Condors lay their eggs where other animals can't reach them.

Can you find these things on the maps?

bald eagle

Mount Everest

yak

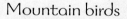

chamois

Ural owl

Rivers and lakes

These people are using reed boats to cross Lake Titicaca.

The dark blue lines and shading on the maps show where rivers and lakes are. The water in them comes from rain and melted snow. Many towns are built near rivers and lakes and lots of animals live in and near them.

A mountain lake

The highest lake in the world is Lake Titicaca, in South America. People there make boats from reeds that grow around the lake.

A river's journey

Rivers start high up in mountains, and flow downhill into lakes or the sea. The water slowly wears away the rock to make a dip in the ground, called a valley.

The Colorado River, in the USA, flows through the world's deepest valley. It is called the Grand Canyon.

A holy river

For many people, the Ganges River, in India, is a holy place. People from around the world go there to bathe in its water.

The water in a waterfall flows fast, and looks white and frothy.

People bathe in the Ganges River during religious festivals.

A waterfall

When a river flows over a steep step in the land, the water tumbles down it and makes a waterfall.

Muddy mouths

The wide, muddy place where a river joins the sea is called the river mouth. Lots of birds live there because the mud is full of plants and tiny fish to eat.

Crocodiles and herons live by the river mouth of the Nile, in Egypt.

Can you spot these things on the maps?

capybara

piranha

Caspian seal

hippopotamus

felucca boat

Seas and oceans

A large group of fish is called a school.

More than half of the Earth is covered with the salty water of seas and oceans. There are five large oceans and lots of smaller seas. They are shown in blue on the maps.

Sea life

Different types of animals and plants live in different parts of the sea. Giant squid live deep under the sea, but crabs and shrimps live in shallow water, near the shore.

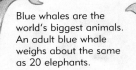

Blue whales are the world's biggest animals. An adult blue whale weighs about the same as 20 elephants.

Some fishing boats have huge nets to catch fish.

Fishing

People catch fish to eat or sell. Some use fishing rods, but most fishermen go out to sea with large nets to catch lots of fish at once.

Can you find these things on the maps?

red snappers   butterfly fish   green turtles   scuba diver   seahorses

Tropical reefs

Coral reefs look like sea plants. In fact, they are made of thousands of tiny animals, called corals. The Great Barrier Reef, near Australia, is the biggest coral reef in the world.

Coral reefs are found in warm, shallow seas. Lots of tropical fish live there too.

Wind surfers use sails to make their boards go faster.

Sea sports

Many people enjoy swimming or splashing around near the seashore. Others go surfing on big waves, or diving under the water to look at fish.

Shipping ports

Ports are towns by the sea where ships are loaded and unloaded. Huge ships carry all kinds of things, such as food and fuel, all around the world.

Big cranes load and unload ships.

common dolphins   marlin   giant squid   shrimps   blue shark

The world

The world is divided into seven large areas called continents. They are all named in big letters on this map.

The little pictures on this map show some world records.

Arctic Circle

Giant redwoods are the tallest trees.

NORTH AMERICA

Blue whales are the biggest animals.

The fastest bird is the peregrine falcon.

Bee hummingbirds are the tiniest birds.

The Sa the w biggest

The Equator is a line added to the maps to show where the middle of the Earth is.

Equator

The biggest insect is the goliath beetle.

The highest waterfall is the Angel Falls.

PACIFIC OCEAN

ATLANTIC OCEAN

Andes Mountains

SOUTH AMERICA

The Andes is the world's longest mountain range.

NORTH

WEST — EAST

SOUTH

There is a compass like this on most maps in this atlas. It shows which way north, south, east and west are.

Antarctic Circle

28

The shading on the maps shows what the land is like in different parts of the world and where there are rivers, lakes, seas and oceans.

ice and snow   deserts   grasslands   forests   mountains   rivers and lakes   seas and oceans

Arctic Circle

ASIA

The Trans-Siberian Express goes along the longest train line.

EUROPE

Mount Everest is the highest mountain.

PACIFIC OCEAN

ARABIAN DESERT

The Nile is the longest river.

AFRICA

More people live in China than in any other country.

Whale sharks are the biggest fish.

Cheetahs are the fastest land animals.

Northeast India is the rainiest place in the world.

Rafflesias are the biggest flowers.

Equator

INDIAN OCEAN

Giraffes are the tallest animals.

Uluru (Ayers Rock) is the largest rock in the world.

The biggest bird is the ostrich.

AUSTRALASIA AND OCEANIA

Antarctic Circle

Antarctica is the world's coldest place.

ANTARCTICA

29

North America

ARCTIC OCEAN

Arctic Circle

Greenland

Nuuk (Godthåb)

Inuit people

Canada goose

minke whale

fishing boat

Labrador dog

puffins

harp seal

cod

ptarmigan

igloo

Paper is made here.

maple

boy in a kayak

snowy owl

harp seal cubs

beluga whale

cloudberries

Hudson Bay

skunk

Arctic terns

wolf

beaver

Arctic hare

muskox

moose

combine harvester

polar bear

icebreaker ship

husky dog

grizzly bear

CANADA

mounted policeman

ice hockey player

Missouri River

arctic char

snow goose

muskrat

lumberjack (forester)

skier

bald eagle

Alaska (USA)

caribou

Rocky Mountains

traditional carved pole

Vancouver

Seattle

raccoon

snowmobile

Anchorage

Gulf of Alaska

Pacific salmon

killer whale

Golden Gate bridge

PACIFIC OCEAN

walrus

OF AMERICA

ATLANTIC OCEAN

Grand Canyon
Colorado
Los Angeles
Cars are made here.
Niagara Falls
New York
Statue of Liberty
Washington DC
The White House
cotton plant
peanuts
crab
tug boat
cargo ship
jumbo jet plane
marlin
stingrays
cruise ship
Leeward Islands
Windward Islands
TRINIDAD AND TOBAGO
NORTH
EAST
SOUTH
WEST
Puerto Rico
carnival dancer
bananas
DOMINICAN REPUBLIC
HAITI
Caribbean monk seal
angel fish
Panama City
PANAMA
howler monkey
PACIFIC OCEAN
giant tortoise
Galápagos Islands (South America)
sea turtle
Coffee is grown here.
San José
COSTA RICA
Managua
NICARAGUA
Tegucigalpa
HONDURAS
San Salvador
EL SALVADOR
Guatemala City
GUATEMALA
Belmopan
BELIZE
Mayan temple
parrot
red snappers
hot peppers
monarch butterfly
Mexico City
cow
donkey
Mexican singer
gila monster
cactus
prickly pear
rattlesnake
Rio Grande River
MEXICO
oil tanker
jazz musician
Mississippi River
paddle steamer
American football player
Hopi dancer
cowboy
elephant seal
great white shark
common dolphins
space agency
oranges
alligator
Havana
CUBA
THE BAHAMAS
scuba diver
reggae singer
JAMAICA
Caribbean Sea
Gulf of Mexico

The world

NORTH AMERICA

This map shows where North America is.

South America

NORTH EAST WEST SOUTH

Equator

white shark

Caribbean Sea

oil rig

Caracas ■

VENEZUELA

iguana

puma

hummingbird

Bogota ■

peccary

COLOMBIA

tapir

Quito ■

ECUADOR

fruit bat

shrimps

Equator

scarlet ibis

Georgetown ■

Paramaribo ■ Cayenne ■

SURINAME FRENCH
GUIANA

GUYANA

rocket base

Angel Falls

Orinoco River

cow

arrow-poison frog

jaguar

Coffee is grown here.

brazil nuts

condor

PERU

Lima ■

Andes Mountains

sardines

caiman

sloth

Amazon River

piranha

Madeira River

Amazon Rainforest

spider monkey

llama

Machu Picchu

reed boat on Lake Titicaca

capybara

armadillo

toucan

blue morpho butterfly

orchid

parrot

Tapajos River

spectacled bear

La Paz ■

BOLIVIA

girl in

bananas

conga drummer

cotton plant

Gold is mined here.

sugar cane

São Francisco River

Tocantins River

Brasilia Cathedral

Brasilia ■

BRAZIL

anaconda

Diamonds are

peanuts

lobster

cocoa beans

Coffee is

Guarani

32

sardines

ATLANTIC OCEAN

oil tanker

mackerel

South Georgia

The world

SOUTH AMERICA

This map shows where South America is.

carnival dancers

surfer

oranges

sardines

Montevideo

URUGUAY

sheep ranches

Buenos Aires

tango dancers

Asunción

giant anteater

Paraná River

gaucho (cowboy)

rhea

ARGENTINA

albatrosses

Falkland Islands

sea lions

Magellan penguin

Cape Horn

chinchilla

...cama Desert

guanaco

Andes Mountains

sheep

flamingos

CHILE

Santiago

grapes

monkey puzzle tree

rockhopper penguin

fur seal

pelican

fishing boat

PACIFIC OCEAN

southern right whale

mackerel

killer whale

33

Australasia and Oceania

PACIFIC OCEAN

NORTH
WEST   EAST
SOUTH

Northern
Mariana Islands

Moorish
idol

FEDERATED
STATES OF
MICRONESIA

PALAU

sea
cucumber

Equator

sacred
house

crowned
pigeon

tree
kangaroo

CUSCUS

dugong

PAPUA
NEW GUINEA

Port Moresby

clown fi

pineapple
fish

box
jellyfish

Great Barrier Reef

coral

harlequin
fish

Aboriginal
dancer

possum

butte
fish

spiny
anteater

frilled lizard

dingo

koalas

boy
diving for
pearls

Great Sandy Desert

AUSTRALIA

wallaby

thorny devil

Uluru
(Ayers Rock)

kangaroos

blue-rin
octop

bottlenose
dolphin

grass
tree

Opals are
mined here.

Darling River

platypus

Sydney
Opera
House

flying
doctor

Great Victoria
Desert

wombat

parakeet

Sydney

blue-tongued
skink

emu

sheep

Canberra

Perth

galah

black
swan

Melbourne

surfer

sea dragon

crayfish

great white
shark

Tasmania

Tasmanian
devil

INDIAN
OCEAN

albatrosses

34

sea slug

Hawaiian Islands

girl wearing a garland

surfer

jumbo jet plane

PACIFIC OCEAN

fairy terns

.RSHALL LANDS

angel fish

cargo ship

URU.

moray eel

blue shark

Equator

green turtles

KIRIBATI

flying fish

LOMON LANDS

parrot fish

Tokelau

UATU

coconut palms

TUVALU

SAMOA American Samoa

manta rays

fisherman in a canoe

Wallis and Futuna

rugby player

coconuts

tuna

.ands

New ledonia

FIJI

TONGA

Niue

sea horses

French Polynesia

bananas

snappers

swordfish

Cook Islands

Tahiti

barracudas

giant squid

The world

kiwi

Maori dancer

NEW .ALAND

Wellington

AUSTRALASIA AND OCEANIA

This map shows where Australasia and Oceania are.

.ep

hoki fish

sperm whale

Asia

Arctic Circle

herring

fishing through ice

kittiwake

lynx

reindeer

Moscow

Volga River

Ural Mountains

RUSSIA

golden eagle

maize

honeybees

noctule bat

flying squirrel

Blue Mosque

Istanbul

Black Sea

Ankara

skier

Astana

saiga antelope

KAZAKHSTAN

space agency

Turkish kebabs

GEORGIA

Caspian Sea

Caspian seal

Aral Sea

wheat

jerboa

Ga
De

TURKEY

ARMENIA

AZERBAIJAN

UZBEKISTAN

Bishkek

KYRGYZSTAN

Cyprus

SYRIA

LEBANON

ISRAEL

Damascus

TURKMENISTAN

Ashgabat

Tashkent

TAJIKISTAN

jackal

snow leopard

Great W of Chin

Jerusalem

IRAQ

Tehran

AFGHANISTAN

Tibetan monks

JORDAN

Baghdad

IRAN

Kabul

Islamabad

The Himalayas

KUWAIT

date palms

Afghan hound

PAKISTAN

New Delhi

NEPAL

Kathmandu

Mount Everest

BHUTAN

hyena

oil well

Bedouin people

QATAR

UNITED ARAB EMIRATES

Muscat

Indus River

Ganges River

BANGLADESH

Mecca

Riyadh

water towers

SAUDI ARABIA

OMAN

girl in a sari

sitar player

Taj Mahal in Agra

INDIA

Bengal tiger

Dhaka

BURMA

boy o eleph

Sana

YEMEN

Arabian horse

Arabian camel

Arabian Sea

Bombay

rickshaw

Rangoon

NORTH

WEST

EAST

SOUTH

Socotra

Arabian fishing boats

sacred cow

tea plant

Andaman Islands

Bang

floatin marke

Sri Jayewardenepura Kotte

SRI LANKA

Colombo

Kuala Lu

Equator

oil tanker

Maldives

rhino

coral reef

snappers

soldier fish

INDIAN OCEAN

tiger shark

36

beluga whale

narwhal

polar bears

ringed seal

walrus

snow goose

snowmobile

bearded seal

Bering Sea

giant kelp forest

bowhead whales

mming

own ear

Siberian tiger

Sea of Okhotsk

sea lion

fishing boat

wild mushrooms

Trans-Siberian Express

ger (tent)

an Bator

GOLIA

Kites are made here.

crested puffin

girl in a kimono

Forbidden City

Vladivostock

NORTH KOREA

Beijing

Pyongyang

Seoul

SOUTH KOREA

JAPAN

Tokyo

bullet train

PACIFIC OCEAN

sperm whale

pollock

puffer fish

white-sided dolphin

acotta rmy

rice plants

CHINA

Yangtze River

crane

sumo wrestler

traditional junk (boat)

bamboo

pagoda

Taipei

TAIWAN

octopus

AM

Hanoi

Hong Kong

South China Sea

dugong

Philippine Sea

iane

AND

Manila

The world

ODIA

basket boat

THE PHILIPPINES

manta ray

ASIA

SIA

BRUNEI

PORE

Barneo

pineapples

giant clam

This map shows where Asia is.

Equator

orang utan

INDONESIA

Jakarta

Java

temple

rafflesia flower

coconut palms

EAST TIMOR

cowrie shells

rubber trees

New Guinea

Arafura Sea

a

37

Africa

Madeira · Rabat · lemons · Algiers ■ · Tunis ■ · TUNISIA · Tripoli ■

Atlas Mountains · olives · spi

Canary Islands · MOROCCO · Berber people · oasis · LIBYA

ATLANTIC OCEAN

Laayoune ■ · ground squirrel · ALGERIA · Sahara Desert · desert

WESTERN SAHARA · date palm

bottlenose dolphin · MAURITANIA · Nouakchott ■ · MALI · camel train · scorpion

fisherman

CAPE VERDE ISLANDS

SENEGAL · Dakar ■ · baboon · hippopotamus · Niger River · NIGER · Niamey ■ · round houses · Ndjar

THE GAMBIA · GUINEA-BISSAU · GUINEA · Bamako ■ · BURKINA FASO · BENIN · Abuja ■

Conakry ■ · bananas · cocoa beans · TOGO · NIGERIA · Lagos ● · bee-eater

Freetown ■ · SIERRA LEONE · Monrovia ■ · Yamoussoukro ■ · Accra ■ · Yaounde ■ · Bar

cargo ship · LIBERIA · IVORY COAST · GHANA · CAMEROON · CON

conger eel · EQUATORIAL GUINEA · Libreville ■ · GABON · Braz

Equator

ATLANTIC OCEAN

flying fish · chimpanzee · ANGOL · Luanda ■ · Ki

oryx

meerkats

The world

AFRICA

This map shows where Africa is.

cruise ship · anchovies · NA · Windhoe

great white shark

38

fishing boat

Cairo

pyramids
EGYPT

Nile River

felucca
boat

Red Sea

*Nubian
Desert*

gourd

crocodile

ERITREA

Khartoum

Asmara

ETHIOPIA

SUDAN

Addis
Ababa

DJIBOUTI

hoopoe

tortoise

acacia
tree

rhinoceros

sugar
cane

lobelia

SOMALIA

Mogadishu

coconut
palms

Arab fishing
boats

INDIAN
OCEAN

NORTH

WEST   EAST

SOUTH

UGANDA

Kampala

*Lake
Victoria*

zebra

coffee
beans

cow fish

Equator

Congo River

KENYA

Nairobi

RWANDA

BURUNDI

lion

Zanzibar
butterfly fish

frigate bird

TANZANIA

Dodoma

Dar es Salaam

SEYCHELLES

hammerhead
shark

mandrill

cloves

DEMOCRATIC
REPUBLIC OF THE
CONGO

vulture

cheetah

African
elephant

MALAWI

oriental
sweetlips fish

ZAMBIA

Lilongwe

Lusaka

Zambezi River

aardvark

aye-aye

ZIMBABWE

Harare

baobab
tree

Antananarivo

Victoria Falls

MOZAMBIQUE

MADAGASCAR

MAURITIUS

BOTSWANA

*Kalahari
Desert*

octopus

Gaborone

sunbird

Pretoria

Johannesburg

Maputo

Bloemfontein

Zulu dancer

SWAZILAND

ring-tailed
lemur

LESOTHO

jellyfish

SOUTH
AFRICA

39

Europe

ARCTIC OCEAN

Arctic Circle

killer whale

ICELAND
Reykjavik■
hot mud pool

ATLANTIC OCEAN

blue whale

humpback whale

cod

Faroe Islands

Shetland Islands

oil rig

fjor

skier

NORWAY
Oslo■

wooden church

salmon

NORTH
WEST EAST
SOUTH

fishing boat

highland piper

gannets

DENMARK
Copenhager

UNITED KINGDOM

North Sea

Irish dancer

Dublin■
IRELAND

sheep

pig

win

Stonehenge

Big Ben

NETHERLANDS
Amsterdam

cargo ship

ferry

Eden project

London■

The Hague

Brussels■

BELGIUM

Cars a made he

GERMANY
LUXEMBOURG Pra

apples

Paris■
Eiffel Tower

grapes

Berns
SWITZERLAND

cas
Al

mussels

FRANCE

oysters

Bay of Biscay

croissants

The Alps

ITALY

SL

art gallery in Bilbao

lavender

skier

PORTUGAL

Leaning Tower of Pisa

Ro

Belem Tower

Madrid■

Corsica

go in

Lisbon■

cork oak tree

SPAIN

bull fighter

church in Barcelona

cruise ship

Sardinia

St Pet the Vo

swordfish

oranges

flamenco dancer

Balearic Islands

sardines

grapes

Mediterranean Sea

Sicily

Madeira

Canary Islands

Saami people

flounder

fishing through ice

Arctic hare

puffins

capercaillie

reindeer

wolverine

Ural Mountains

Siberian chipmunk

SWEDEN

wild mushrooms

FINLAND

sparrow hawk

Ural owl

Baltic Sea

lynx

sable

ballet dancers

wheat

sprats

Helsinki

Stockholm

Tallinn

ESTONIA

Paper is made here.

beaver

RUSSIA

Winter Palace in St. Petersburg

gymnast

LATVIA

Riga

cow

red fox

Moscow St. Basil's Cathedral

maize

Volga River

LITHUANIA

Vilnius

potatoes

wild horses

ships are made here.

Minsk

BELARUS

Russian dolls

black stork

POLAND

Warsaw

wild boar

European bison

deer

Kiev

Dnieper River

Don River

balalaika player

Caspian Sea

brown bear

chamois

UKRAINE

Cossack dancer

Carpathian Mountains

MOLDOVA

SLOVAKIA

Bratislava

Chisinau

sunflowers

Budapest

HUNGARY

castle

ROMANIA

space telescope

The world

Belgrade

Bucharest

SERBIA & MONTENEGRO

Danube River

Black Sea

sturgeon

EUROPE

fortress in Dubrovnik

SERBIA & MONTENEGRO

Sofia

BULGARIA

grapes

MACEDONIA

Istanbul

ALBANIA

TURKEY

This map shows where Europe is.

GREECE

Athens

Parthenon

Crete

olives

fishing boat

The Arctic

Bering Sea

Gulf of Alaska

fishing boat

volcanoes

Sea of Okhotsk

walrus

Alaska (USA)

bearded seal

Chukchi tent

snowmobile

husky racer

moose

Chukchi Sea

Wrangel Island

Siberian tiger

wolf

Beaufort Sea

polar bear

salmon

Arctic loon

purple heron

RUSSIA

CANADA

ARCTIC OCEAN

New Siberia Islands

Laptev Sea

snowy owl

Canada goose

Arctic fox

Arctic terns

narwhal

lynx

stoat

Arctic hare

helicopter

Severnaya Zemlya

lemming

Ellesmere Island

ringed seal

North Pole

Kara Sea

Baffin Island

Arctic poppies

Arctic chars

caribou

polar bear

explorer

Franz Josef Land

Novaya Zemlya

GREENLAND

harp seal

satellite station

Svalbard

Barents Sea

Arctic Circle

boy in a kayak

Nuuk (Godthab)

musk ox

minke whale

ptarmigan

Reykjavik

ICELAND

puffins

cod

ATLANTIC OCEAN

fishing boat

ferry

The world

THE ARCTIC

ANTARCTICA

The Arctic and Antarctica are on opposite sides of the world.

42

Antarctica

South Georgia

Africa is this way.

sea bass

blue whale

ATLANTIC OCEAN

SOUTHERN OCEAN

wandering albatrosses

krill

snail fish

cruise ship

Weddell Sea

robot submarine

macaroni penguin

scientist with a weather balloon

Adelie penguins

INDIAN OCEAN

British science station

leopard seal

Ronne Ice Shelf

Antarctic Peninsula

South Africa is this way.

ANTARCTICA

Weddell seal

fur seal

American science station

South Pole

caterpillar truck

rockhopper penguin

chinstrap penguin

Transantarctic Mountains

brittle star

gentoo penguins

snowmobile

ski plane

elephant seal

Antarctic Circle

Ross Ice Shelf

Australian science station

krill

emperor penguins

Ross Sea

king penguin

French science station

giant petrels

ice fish

soft coral

blue-eyed shag

cod

PACIFIC OCEAN

salmon shark

SOUTHERN OCEAN

krill

Australia is this way.

Arctic terns

killer whale

43

A trip around the world

Are you ready for a trip around the world?
Look back through this book and try this
fun quiz to find out. The answers
are all on page 48.

Packing your bags

You'll need to pack
carefully for your trip.
Can you match
these things to the
places where
you'll need them?

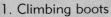

1. Climbing boots
2. A warm coat
3. A water bottle
4. A diving suit

a. The Arctic
b. Mount Everest
c. The Atacama Desert
d. The Great Barrier Reef

Things to see

1. Would you see
penguins in the Arctic or
in Antarctica?

2. In which town in Italy
would you see canals
instead of roads?

3. Which is the only
country where you can
see koalas and
kangaroos in the wild?

4. Which city in Brazil
would you visit to see
people dressed up for
a carnival?

Country shapes

Here are the shapes of some of the countries you might visit. Can you recognize them from the maps?

4.

1.
2.
3.

Blue clues

Can you find and name all of these things with "blue" in their names?

1. A butterfly that lives in the Amazon rainforest.

2. An octopus that swims near Australia.

3. An Australian lizard with an unusual tongue.

4. A North American bird.

People to meet

In which countries would you expect to meet these people?

1. Hopi dancer
2. Girl in a kimono
3. Reggae singer
4. Zulu dancer

Index of places

Index of things

Answers

Things to spot

Countries and cities
Big Ben, 40
Parthenon, 41
St. Basil's Cathedral, 41
Forbidden City, 37
Eiffel Tower, 40
Blue Mosque, 36
Winter Palace in St. Petersburg, 41
Leaning Tower of Pisa, 40
Sydney Opera House, 34
Statue of Liberty, 31

People
Guarani people, 32
Zulu dancer, 39
sitar player, 36
rugby player, 35
highland piper, 40
conga drummer, 32
Tibetan monks, 36
Hopi dancer, 31
girl in a poncho, 32
American football player, 31

Getting around
basket boat, 37
desert truck, 38
traditional junk (boat), 37
Trans-Siberian Express, 29, 37
helicopter, 42

Ice and snow
ice fish, 43
humpback whale, 40
American science station, 43
Arctic fox, 42
Saami people, 41

Deserts
fennec fox, 39
jerboa, 36
blue-tongued skink, 34
scorpion, 38
rattlesnake, 31

Grasslands
kangaroos, 34
guanaco, 33
buffalo, 30
giraffe, 39
meerkats, 38

lion, 39
giant anteater, 33
African elephant, 39
oryx, 38
rhea, 33

Forests
blue morpho butterfly, 32
armadillo, 32
red fox, 41
raccoon, 30
anaconda, 32
grizzly bear, 30
wild mushrooms, 37
lumberjack (forester), 30
chimpanzee, 38
toucan, 32

Mountains
bald eagle, 30
Mount Everest, 29, 36
yak, 36
chamois, 41
Ural owl, 41

Rivers and lakes
capybara, 32
piranha, 32

Caspian seal, 36
hippopotamus, 38
felucca boat, 39

Seas and oceans
red snappers, 31
butterfly fish, 34
green turtles, 35
scuba diver, 31
seahorses, 35
common dolphins, 31
marlin, 31
giant squid, 35
shrimps, 32
blue shark, 35

A trip around the world

Packing your bags
1. b. You'll need climbing boots on Mount Everest.
2. a. A warm coat will keep out the cold in the Arctic.
3. c. The Atacama Desert is the driest place on Earth, so you'll need a water bottle.

4. d. You'll need a diving suit to dive down to the Great Barrier Reef.

Places to see
1. Antarctica
2. Venice
3. Australia
4. Rio de Janeiro

Country shapes
1. New Zealand
2. Mexico
3. Australia
4. Italy

Blue clues
1. Blue morpho butterfly
2. Blue-ringed octopus
3. Blue-tongued skink
4. Blue jay

People to meet
1. USA
2. Japan
3. Jamaica
4. South Africa

Managing editor: Gillian Doherty   Managing designer: Russell Punter

The publishers are grateful to the following organizations and individuals for their permission to reproduce material. **p6** This image is an extract from the Millennium Map™ which is
© getmapping.com plc; **p7** ©Tom Van Sant; Geosphere Project/Planetary Visions/Science Photo Library